DANGEROUS JOURNEYS

EXPLORING THE DEEP SEA

BY ALLAN MOREY

TORQUE™

BELLWETHER MEDIA · MINNEAPOLIS, MN

™

Torque brims with excitement
perfect for thrill-seekers of all kinds.
Discover daring survival skills, explore
uncharted worlds, and marvel at mighty
engines and extreme sports. In *Torque* books,
anything can happen. Are you ready?

This edition first published in 2023 by Bellwether Media, Inc.

No part of this publication may be reproduced in whole or in part without
written permission of the publisher. For information regarding permission,
write to Bellwether Media, Inc., Attention: Permissions Department,
6012 Blue Circle Drive, Minnetonka, MN 55343.

Library of Congress Cataloging-in-Publication Data

LC record for Exploring the Deep Sea available at:
https://lccn.loc.gov/2022012986

Text copyright © 2023 by Bellwether Media, Inc. TORQUE and associated
logos are trademarks and/or registered trademarks of Bellwether Media, Inc.

Editor: Kieran Downs   Designer: Josh Brink

Printed in the United States of America, North Mankato, MN.

TABLE OF CONTENTS

THE MARIANA TRENCH

A small **submersible** dives down into the Mariana **Trench**. This long **crevasse** lies along the Pacific Ocean floor. At nearly 7 miles (11 kilometers) deep, it is the deepest spot in the world.

SUBMERSIBLE

TALLEST VERSUS DEEPEST

THE MARIANA TRENCH IS MORE THAN 7,000 FEET (2,134 METERS) DEEPER THAN MOUNT EVEREST IS TALL!

Darkness surrounds the submersible. But its lights reveal strange creatures swimming about. There is much to explore at the bottom of the ocean!

INTO THE DEEP

Any dive of 60 feet (18 meters) or more is a deep dive. At this depth, the weight of the water can damage a person's heart and lungs.

DEEP DIVE

AHMED GABR HOLDS THE WORLD
RECORD FOR THE DEEPEST DIVE BY
A HUMAN WITHOUT A SUBMERSIBLE.
HE DOVE ABOUT 1,090 FEET
(332 METERS) INTO
THE RED SEA!

At 3,281 feet (1,000 meters), the ocean goes dark. No sunlight can reach this depth. No plants can grow. Temperatures drop near freezing.

Submersibles help people reach the deep sea. They protect people from the water's crushing weight and cold temperatures.

In 1934, the *Bathysphere* submersible first reached 3,000 feet (914 meters). In 1960, the *Trieste* dove into Challenger Deep. At nearly 36,000 feet (10,973 meters), this is the deepest part of the Mariana Trench.

BATHYSPHERE

MARIANA TRENCH MAP

MARIANA TRENCH = ◆

CHALLENGER DEEP = ◇

SHIPWRECK

Scientists journey down into the deep sea for **research**. They learn about the strange wildlife living there. They map the ocean floor. They also discover old shipwrecks.

Scientists study how people affect the ocean. They have found trash in the deepest parts of the ocean.

NOTABLE EXPLORER

NAME: SYLVIA EARLE

BORN: AUGUST 30, 1935

JOURNEY: IN 1979, WALKED UNTETHERED ALONG THE OCEAN FLOOR WHILE WEARING A SPECIAL DIVING SUIT

RESULTS: SET A WORLD RECORD FOR EXPLORING THE OCEAN FLOOR AT A DEPTH OF 1,250 FEET (380 METERS)

PLANNING AND PREPARATION

Training is important for any deep-sea dive. People learn to pilot a submersible. They also learn what to do in case of an emergency.

People do safety checks before the journey. They test **communication devices**. They charge **batteries**. They make sure there is enough power for the trip.

Breathable air is important when traveling underwater. Submersibles carry **oxygen** tanks. The tanks hold enough air for several hours.

As people breathe, they make **carbon dioxide** (CO2). Too much of this gas can be poisonous. Submersibles have air scrubbers. These remove CO2 from the air. This allows passengers to breathe safely.

PLANNING YOUR JOURNEY

LEARN TO PILOT

CHECK EQUIPMENT

FILL OXYGEN TANKS

PACK SUPPLIES

DIVING DOWN

Deep-sea journeys start with a boat ride. The submersible is carried to the dive site. A **crane** lowers it into the water.

CRANE

ANGLERFISH

NIGHT LIGHTS

SOME DEEP-SEA CREATURES CREATE THEIR OWN LIGHT. THIS HELPS THEM SEE IN THE DARK!

Ballast tanks are used to change the depth of the submersible. The tanks fill with water to dive down. They fill with air to rise up.

HULL

Nuytco Research

6

NEWTSUB
DeepWorker

As the submersible dives deeper, water puts **pressure** on it. Thick metal **hulls** keep the passengers safe. The hulls are built to hold up to a lot of pressure.

Deep-sea waters are cold. Heaters keep passengers warm. The deep sea is also dark. Lights on the outside of the craft let passengers see.

DEEP SEA DIVING WITHOUT A SUBMERSIBLE

UNABLE TO SEE

LUNGS COLLAPSE FROM WATER PRESSURE

RUN OUT OF OXYGEN

BODY FREEZES

MECHANICAL CLAW

Scientists sometimes collect **samples** when they reach the ocean floor. They use a **mechanical** claw to pick up objects. This claw is controlled by a **joystick**.

Going to the bottom of the ocean is dangerous. But it is a place of strange wildlife and amazing landscapes. There is much to explore in the deep sea!

GLOSSARY

ballast tanks—large parts on submersibles that hold water or air

batteries—parts of a submersible that give it power

carbon dioxide—a gas that humans create when they breathe out

communication devices—tools that allow people to talk with each other from a distance

crane—a machine used for raising and lowering heavy objects

crevasse—a large, deep crack

hulls—the bodies of watercraft

joystick—a stick used to control something larger

mechanical—having to do with machines or engines

oxygen—a gas needed to breathe

pressure—the force put on an object or person

research—careful study of a subject

samples—small amounts of dirt, rock, and other materials that give information about where they were taken from

submersible—a craft built for traveling underwater

trench—a long ditch or crack in the seafloor

TO LEARN MORE

AT THE LIBRARY

Colins, Luke. *Underwater Robots*. Mankato, Minn.: Black Rabbit Books, 2020.

Cusolito, Michelle. *Diving Deep: Using Machines to Explore the Ocean*. Watertown, Mass.: Charlesbridge, 2022.

Mattern, Joanne. *Submarines and Submersibles*. Vero Beach, Fla.: Rourke Educational Media, 2019.

ON THE WEB

FACTSURFER

Factsurfer.com gives you a safe, fun way to find more information.

1. Go to www.factsurfer.com

2. Enter "exploring the deep sea" into the search box and click 🔍.

3. Select your book cover to see a list of related content.

INDEX

The images in this book are reproduced through the courtesy of: Wild Horizon/ Getty Images, front cover (hero), pp. 10, 14, 20; Osman Temizel, cover, CIP (background), p. 23; Xinhua/ Alamy, pp. 4, 16; NOAA Okeanos Explorer/ wiki commons, p. 5; Science History Images/ Alamy, p. 6; Laura Dts, p. 7; Everett Collection/ Alamy, p. 8; Bettmann/ Getty Images, p. 9; Andriy Nekrasov, p. 11; Alain Le Garsmeur Dr Sylvia Earle/ Alamy, p. 11 (Sylvia Earle); chonlasub woravichan, p. 11 (coral); Jeffrey Rotman/ Alamy, p. 12; Stephen Frink Collection/ Alamy, p. 13; Vane Nunes, p. 15 (fill oxygen tank); PJF Military Collection/ Alamy, p. 15 (check equipment); Michael Pitts/ naturepl.com/ Alamy, p. 15 (learn to pilot); David Pereiras, p. 15 (pack supplies); David Shale/ Alamy, p. 17; Kip Evans/ Alamy